Windows!
A Kid's Guide to Rotterdam, Netherlands

Photography by John D. Weigand
Poetry by Penelope Dyan

Bellissima Publishing, LLC
Jamul, California
www.bellissimapublishing.com

Copyright © 2018 by Penny D. Weigand & John D. Weigand

All rights reserved. No part of this book may be reproduced or transmitted in any form or by any means, electronic or mechanical, including photocopying, recording, or by any other means, or by any information or storage retrieval system, without permission from the publisher.

ISBN 978-1-61477-334-4
First Edition

"Some places are built by the circumstances of time."

PENELOPE DYAN

Windows!
Bellissima Publishing, LLC

Introduction

Rotterdam, Netherlands is sometimes called the gateway to Europe, because it is a great port city; and, as they say, location is everything! Rotterdam's history goes back to 1270, when a dam was constructed in the Rotte river, after which people settled around it for safety. Hence, thereafter, the city was called Rotterdam. Even more interesting is that because of its almost complete destruction during what is known as the World War II Rotterdam Blitz, the city had to be rebuilt. And the result was a completely new and modern look that included sky-scrapers, which are an uncommon sight in the Netherlands. And this architecture is why this book (as you will see) is called "Windows!" (Oh, and don't miss its meaning.)

Written by the award winning author, attorney and former teacher, Penelope Dyan, with photography by John D. Weigand, this kid-sized book, perfect for a kid-sized backpack, will help you practice your reading skills; because this is a 'learn to read' book filled with word recognition, word repetition and rhyme.

When you are finished reading, watch the free music video that goes with this book that can be found on Bellissimavideo's YouTube channel! Then you can see even more of Rotterdam!

Windows!
Bellissima Publishing, LLC

Windows!
A Kid's Guide to Rotterdam, Netherlands

Photography by John D. Weigand
Poetry by Penelope Dyan

When you look out your hotel window,
something becomes very clear to you.
Because when you look out
of your hotel window,
you see much more than just a view.

As you go out, you look far and wide,
the diversity of Rotterdam
is something they don't try to hide.

The pointed rooftops and the windows remind you of times long past.

But this old-time conservative look
(and this impression)
does not long last.

You take a closer look.

And you look closer still!
And as the sizes and colors and shapes
of these windows and these buildings
seem to change in afternoon's light,
you wonder how they will look
when these windows are lit and shining
throughout the long night!
The shapes (alone) of these buildings
are different from anything
you have ever, ever seen.
And your dad, contemplating, asks,
"If all art is from the soul
(and this is art)
then what does this art mean?"

You see a water taxi.

You see a bridge and more shapes and more windows still.
And then . . .

Across the water you see even more,
and your dad thinks once again
about this city's soul.
The buildings are fascinating,
and like the mighty Phoenix,
and without any compunction,
this city rose right from the ashes,
of World War II's destruction.

You turn around
and more and more windows you see,
again revealing art's diversity.
And your dad tells you these windows
are more eyes to this city's soul.
And you notice
the eyes of these windows
seem follow you
wherever you go!

If you want to go someplace
by water,
you don't have to fuss.
If you don't want to travel
by water taxi,
you can travel right on the waterbus!

Later, as back to your hotel room
with Mom and Dad you go . . .
with them, you again contemplate
this city's soul.
And you wonder again how and why
the architects used all of those shapes
and colors to reach up to the sky.
You decide that you agree with Dad.
Designing a building
is a true form of art.
And then you stop and you think
about each architect's heart.
Then you decide (as you already know)
that more than just eyes
are the windows to the soul.

"Some things are truly created out of the depths of one's soul."

PENELOPE DYAN